4
american popular piano
ETUDES

Compositions by
Christopher Norton

**Additional Compositions
and Arrangements**
Dr. Scott McBride Smith

Editor
Dr. Scott McBride Smith

Associate Editor
Clarke MacIntosh

Music

Stratford, Ontario, Canada

A Note about this Book

Pop music styles can be grouped into three broad categories:

- **lyrical** — pieces with a beautiful singing quality and rich harmonies; usually played at a slow tempo;

- **rhythmic** — more up-tempo pieces, with energetic, catchy rhythms; these often have a driving left hand part;

- **ensemble** — works meant to be played with other musicians, or with backing tracks (or both!); this type of piece requires careful listening and shared energy.

American Popular Piano has been deliberately designed to develop skills in all three areas.

You can integrate the cool, motivating pieces in **American Popular Piano** into your piano studies in several ways.

- pick a piece you like and learn it; when you're done, pick another!

- choose a piece from each category to develop a complete range of skills in your playing;

- polish a particular favorite for your local festival or competition. Works from **American Popular Piano** are featured on the lists of required pieces for many festivals and competitions;

- use the pieces as optional contemporary selections in music examinations;

- Or...just have fun!

Going hand-in-hand with the repertoire in **American Popular Piano** are the innovative **Etudes Albums** and **Skills Books**, designed to enhance each student's musical experience by building technical and aural skills.

- **Technical Etudes** in both Classical and Pop Styles are based on musical ideas and technical challenges drawn from the repertoire. Practice these to improve your chops!

- **Improvisation Etudes** offer an exciting new approach to improvisation that guides students effortlessly into spontaneous creativity. Not only does the user-friendly module structure integrate smoothly into traditional lessons, it opens up a whole new understanding of the repertoire being studied.

- **Skills Books** help students develop key supporting skills in sight-reading, ear-training and technique; presented in complementary study modules that are both practical and effective.

Use all of the elements of **American Popular Piano** together to incorporate a comprehensive course of study into your everyday routine. The carefully thought-out pacing makes learning almost effortless. Making music and real progress has never been so much fun!

Library and Archives Canada Cataloguing in Publication

Norton, Christopher, 1953-

American popular piano [music] : etudes / compositions by Christopher Norton ;
additional compositions and arrangements, Scott McBride Smith ;
editor, Scott McBride Smith ; associate editor, S. Clarke MacIntosh.

To be complete in 11 volumes.
The series is organized in 11 levels, from preparatory to level 10, each including a repertoire album,
an etudes album, a skills book, and an instrumental backings compact disc.

ISBN 1-897379-11-0 (preparatory level).--ISBN 1-897379-12-9 (level 1).--
ISBN 1-897379-13-7 (level 2).--ISBN 1-897379-14-5 (level 3).--
ISBN 1-897379-15-3 (level 4).--ISBN 1-897379-16-1 (level 5)

1. Piano--Studies and exercises. I. Smith, Scott McBride II. MacIntosh, S. Clarke, 1959- III. Title.

MT225.N883A52 2006   786.2   C2006906214-5

LEVEL 4 ETUDES
Table of Contents

Improv Etude - Rockin' In The Aisles

MODULE 1

A Play the backing track of *Rockin' In The Aisles.* The opening clicks represent ♩ (quarter notes).
After the clicks, clap ♩ with the track.

B Clap with the backing track:

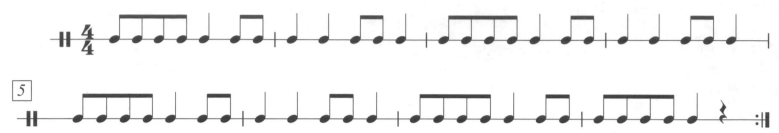

C 1. Play *without* the backing track.
2. Play again *with* the backing track.

D 1. Play *without* the backing track.
2. Play again *with* the backing track.

E 1. Play *without* the backing track.
2. Play again *with* the backing track.

* Improv notes:

* IMPROVISATION:
use this rhythm

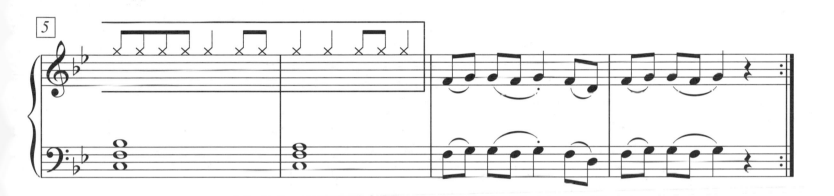

* use the Improv notes in any order

Listen closely as you play your improvisation.
- Does each note sound good with the backing track?
- Are you keeping a steady beat and staying with the backing track?
Play several different improvisations and choose your favorite. Play it for your teacher.

✔ **Improv Tip:** *If you memorize the rhythmic pattern before you start, it will help*
you be more free in your note selection during your improvisation.

4

Improv Etude - Rockin' In The Aisles

MODULE 2

A Play the backing track of *Rockin' In The Aisles*. The opening clicks represent ♩ (quarter notes). After the clicks, clap ♩ with the track.

B Clap with the backing track:

C 1. Play *without* the backing track.
   2. Play again *with* the backing track.

D 1. Play *without* the backing track.
   2. Play again *with* the backing track.

E 1. Play *without* the backing track.
    2. Play again *with* the backing track.

* Improv notes:

* IMPROVISATION:
use this rhythm

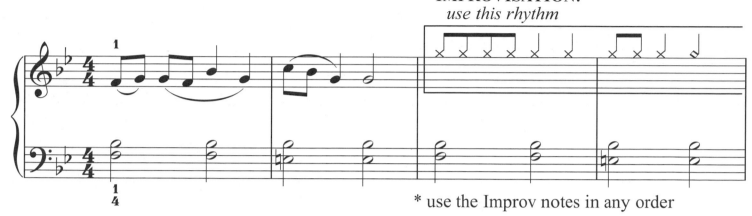

* use the Improv notes in any order

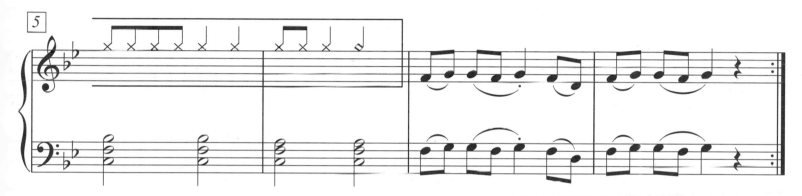

Listen closely as you play your improvisation.
  - Does each note sound good with the backing track?
  - Are you keeping a steady beat and staying with the backing track?
Play several different improvisations and choose your favorite. Play it for your teacher.

✔ Improv Tip: *Rests are an important part of pop style. You can add them to your improvisation.*

6

Improv Etude - Rockin' In The Aisles

MODULE 3

A Play the backing track of *Rockin' In The Aisles.* The opening clicks represent ♩ (quarter notes). After the clicks, clap ♩ with the track.

B Clap with the backing track:

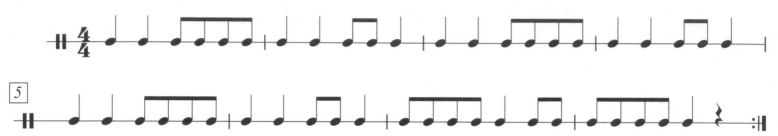

C 1. Play *without* the backing track.
    2. Play again *with* the backing track.

D 1. Play *without* the backing track.
    2. Play again *with* the backing track.

E 1. Play *without* the backing track.
2. Play again *with* the backing track.

* Improv notes:

* IMPROVISATION:
use this rhythm

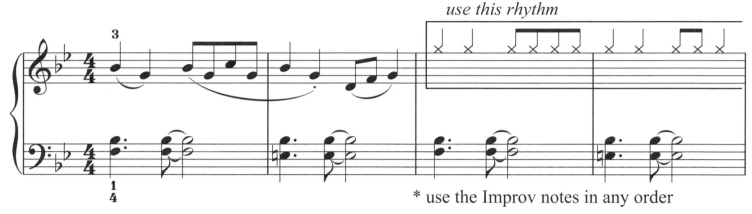

* use the Improv notes in any order

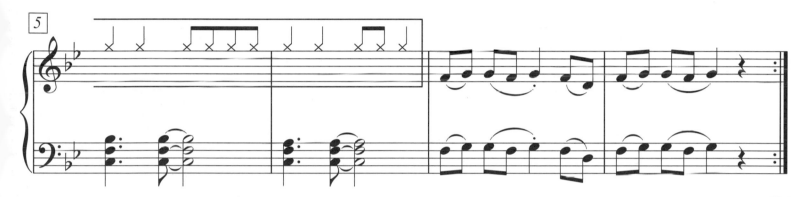

Listen closely as you play your improvisation.
  - Does each note sound good with the backing track?
  - Are you keeping a steady beat and staying with the backing track?
Play several different improvisations and choose your favorite. Play it for your teacher.

✔ Improv Tip: *Do the rhythmic patterns in each measure repeat in other measures?*
Try repeating your melody notes, too - or just changing one.

Improv Etude - Rockin' In The Aisles

8

MODULE 4

A Play the backing track of *Rockin' In The Aisles.* The opening clicks represent ♩ (quarter notes).
After the clicks, clap ♩ with the track.

B Clap with the backing track:

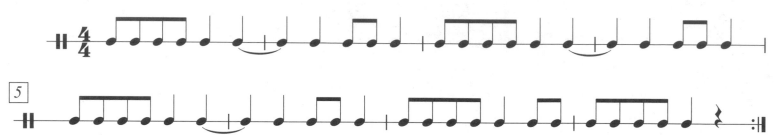

C 1. Play *without* the backing track.
2. Play again *with* the backing track.

D 1. Play *without* the backing track.
2. Play again *with* the backing track.

E 1. Play *without* the backing track.
   2. Play again *with* the backing track.

* Improv notes:

* IMPROVISATION:
use this rhythm

* use the Improv notes in any order

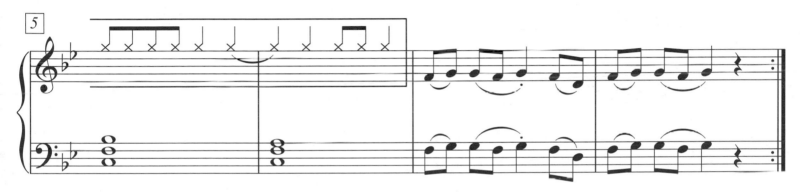

Listen closely as you play your improvisation.
  - Does each note sound good with the backing track?
  - Are you keeping a steady beat and staying with the backing track?
Play several different improvisations and choose your favorite. Play it for your teacher.

✔ **Improv Tip:** *Dynamics and articulation are important for a musical and interesting improvisation.*

Improv Etude - Going For It

MODULE 1

A Play the backing track of *Going For It*. The opening clicks represent ♩ (quarter notes).
After the clicks, clap ♩ with the track.

B Clap with the backing track:

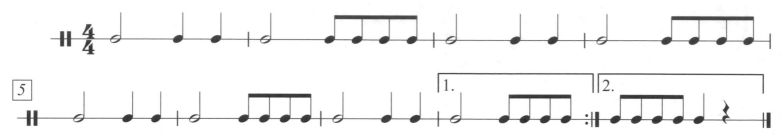

C 1. Play *without* the backing track.
2. Play again *with* the backing track.

D 1. Play *without* the backing track.
2. Play again *with* the backing track.

E 1. Play *without* the backing track.
2. Play again *with* the backing track.

* Improv notes:

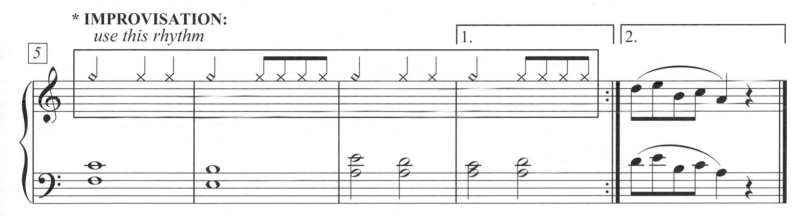

* IMPROVISATION:
use this rhythm

* use the Improv notes in any order

Listen closely as you play your improvisation.
- Does each note sound good with the backing track?
- Are you keeping a steady beat and staying with the backing track?
Play several different improvisations and choose your favorite. Play it for your teacher.

✔ **Improv Tip:** *Are you having trouble staying with the backing?*
Counting out loud is always better than silent counting - or no counting at all!

Improv Etude - Going For It

MODULE 2

A Play the backing track of *Going For It.* The opening clicks represent ♩ (quarter notes).

After the clicks, clap ♩ with the track.

B Clap with the backing track:

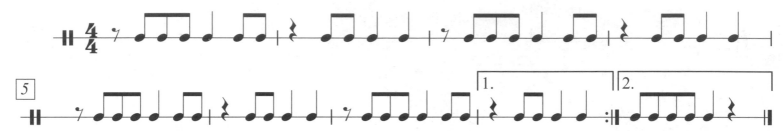

C 1. Play *without* the backing track.
2. Play again *with* the backing track.

D 1. Play *without* the backing track.
2. Play again *with* the backing track.

E 1. Play *without* the backing track.
2. Play again *with* the backing track.

* Improv notes:

* IMPROVISATION:
use this rhythm

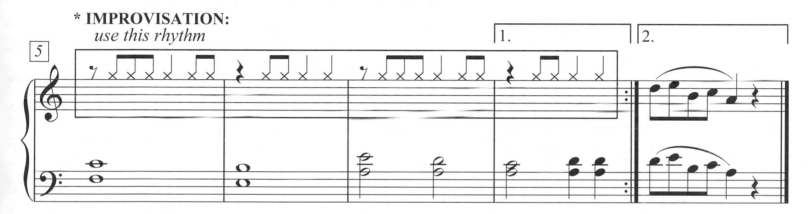

* use the Improv notes in any order

Listen closely as you play your improvisation.
- Does each note sound good with the backing track?
- Are you keeping a steady beat and staying with the backing track?
Play several different improvisations and choose your favorite. Play it for your teacher.

✔ **Improv Tip:** *The rh rhythm is more complicated here. Keep your melodic ideas simple.*

Improv Etude - Going For It

MODULE 3

A Play the backing track of *Going For It*. The opening clicks represent ♩ (quarter notes).
After the clicks, clap ♩ with the track.

B Clap with the backing track:

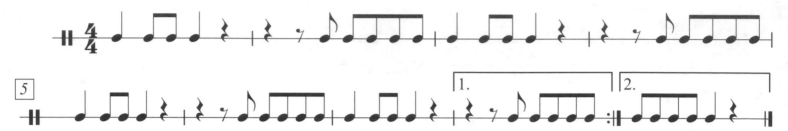

C 1. Play *without* the backing track.
2. Play again *with* the backing track.

D 1. Play *without* the backing track.
2. Play again *with* the backing track.

E 1. Play *without* the backing track.
    2. Play again *with* the backing track.

* Improv notes:

* IMPROVISATION:
use this rhythm

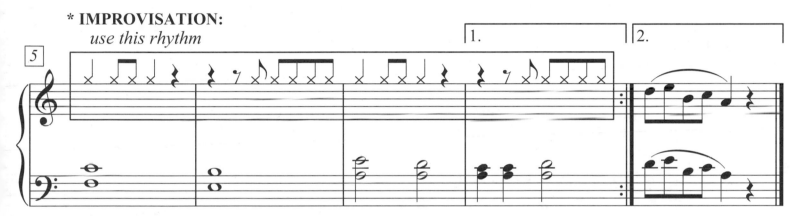

* use the Improv notes in any order

Listen closely as you play your improvisation.
  - Does each note sound good with the backing track?
  - Are you keeping a steady beat and staying with the backing track?
Play several different improvisations and choose your favorite. Play it for your teacher.

✔ **Improv Tip:** *Make sure your rhythm is totally solid.*
                You may have to practice slowly several times.

Improv Etude - Going For It

MODULE 4

A Play the backing track of *Going For It.* The opening clicks represent ♩ (quarter notes).
After the clicks, clap ♩ with the track.

B Clap with the backing track:

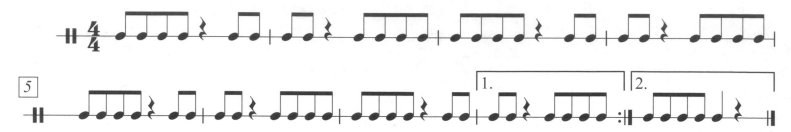

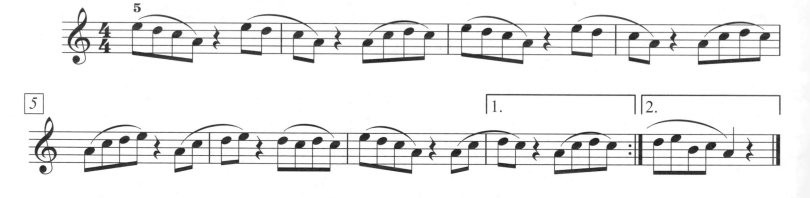

C 1. Play *without* the backing track.
2. Play again *with* the backing track.

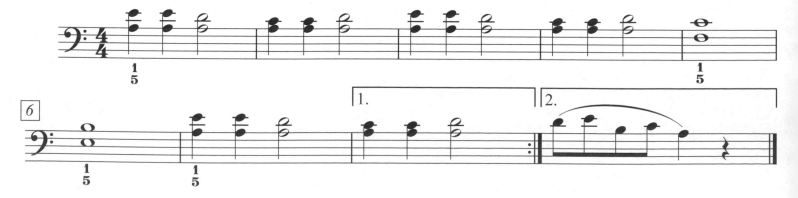

D 1. Play *without* the backing track.
2. Play again *with* the backing track.

E 1. Play *without* the backing track.
2. Play again *with* the backing track.

* Improv notes:

* IMPROVISATION:
use this rhythm

* use the Improv notes in any order

Listen closely as you play your improvisation.
- Does each note sound good with the backing track?
- Are you keeping a steady beat and staying with the backing track?
Play several different improvisations and choose your favorite. Play it for your teacher.

✔ **Improv Tip:** *How many four-note melodic patterns do you see in mm. 1-4?*
Do they always start on the same beat? Invent some four-note melodies of your own.

Improv Etude - A Knight's Tale

MODULE 1

A Play the backing track of *A Knight's Tale*. The opening clicks represent ♩ (quarter notes).
After the clicks, clap ♩ with the track.

B Clap with the backing track:

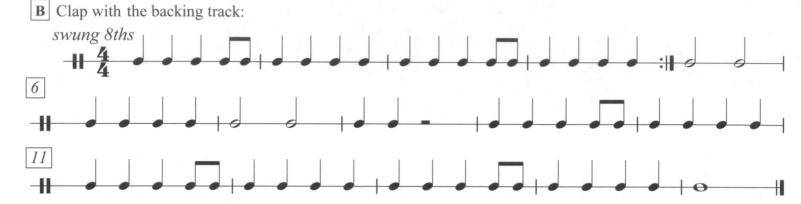

C 1. Play *without* the backing track.
2. Play again *with* the backing track.

D 1. Play *without* the backing track.
2. Play again *with* the backing track.

E 1. Play *without* the backing track.
2. Play again *with* the backing track.

* Improv notes:

swung 8ths

* **IMPROVISATION:** *use this rhythm*

* use the Improv notes in any order

* **IMPROVISATION:** *use this rhythm*

* use the Improv notes in any order

Listen closely as you play your improvisation.
- Does each note sound good with the backing track?
- Are you keeping a steady beat and staying with the backing track?
Play several different improvisations and choose your favorite. Play it for your teacher.

✔ **Improv Tip:** *Rhythm is primary in pop music. Feel the swing before you play.*

Improv Etude - A Knight's Tale

MODULE 2

A Play the backing track of *A Knight's Tale*. The opening clicks represent ♩ (quarter notes).
After the clicks, clap ♩ with the track.

B Clap with the backing track:
swung 8ths

C 1. Play *without* the backing track.
2. Play again *with* the backing track.

swung 8ths

D 1. Play *without* the backing track.
2. Play again *with* the backing track.

E 1. Play *without* the backing track.
2. Play again *with* the backing track.

* Improv notes:

Listen closely as you play your improvisation.
   - Does each note sound good with the backing track?
   - Are you keeping a steady beat and staying with the backing track?
Play several different improvisations and choose your favorite. Play it for your teacher.

✔ **Improv Tip:** *The melody is in the Aeolian mode - A minor with a flat sixth note (F) and flat seventh note (G). Try different arrangements of this mode in your improvisation.*

Improv Etude - A Knight's Tale

MODULE 3

A Play the backing track of *A Knight's Tale*. The opening clicks represent ♩ (quarter notes).

After the clicks, clap ♩ with the track.

B Clap with the backing track:

C 1. Play *without* the backing track.
2. Play again *with* the backing track.

D 1. Play *without* the backing track.
2. Play again *with* the backing track.

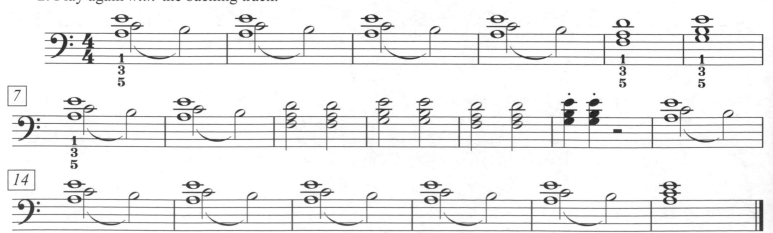

E 1. Play *without* the backing track.
2. Play again *with* the backing track.

* Improv notes:

swung 8ths

* **IMPROVISATION:** *use this rhythm*

* use the Improv notes in any order

* **IMPROVISATION:**
use this rhythm

* usc the Improv notes in any order

Listen closely as you play your improvisation.
   - Does each note sound good with the backing track?
   - Are you keeping a steady beat and staying with the backing track?
Play several different improvisations and choose your favorite. Play it for your teacher.

✔ **Improv Tip:** *Keep the swung eighth notes light and decide what other beats you might*
like to accent in your improvisation. Syncopation is always cool.

Improv Etude - A Knight's Tale

MODULE 4

A Play the backing track of *A Knight's Tale*. The opening clicks represent ♩ (quarter notes).

After the clicks, clap ♩ with the track.

B Clap with the backing track:

C 1. Play *without* the backing track.
2. Play again *with* the backing track.

D 1. Play *without* the backing track.
2. Play again *with* the backing track.

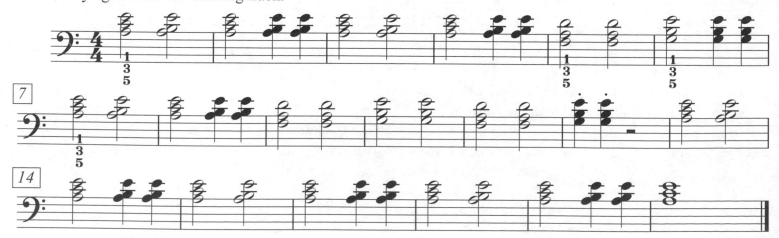

E 1. Play *without* the backing track.
2. Play again *with* the backing track.

* Improv notes:

Listen closely as you play your improvisation.
- Does each note sound good with the backing track?
- Are you keeping a steady beat and staying with the backing track?

Play several different improvisations and choose your favorite. Play it for your teacher.

✔ **Improv Tip:** *Music is boring without dissonance. Try adding some dissonant notes to your improvisation in a few places.*

Improv Etude - Trucking Along

MODULE 1

A Play the backing track of *Trucking Along*. The opening clicks represent ♩ (quarter notes).
After the clicks, clap ♩ with the track.

B Clap with the backing track:

C 1. Play *without* the backing track.
2. Play again *with* the backing track.

D 1. Play *without* the backing track.
2. Play again *with* the backing track.

E 1. Play *without* the backing track.
2. Play again *with* the backing track.

* Improv notes:

swung 8ths

* **IMPROVISATION:**
    use this rhythm

* use the Improv notes in any order

Listen closely as you play your improvisation.
- Does each note sound good with the backing track?
- Are you keeping a steady beat and staying with the backing track?
Play several different improvisations and choose your favorite. Play it for your teacher.

✔ **Improv Tip:** *It can be effective to use only a small group of notes in your improvisation.*
                   Which ones will you take out?

Improv Etude - Trucking Along

MODULE 2

A Play the backing track of *Trucking Along*. The opening clicks represent ♩ (quarter notes).
   After the clicks, clap ♩ with the track.

B Clap with the backing track:

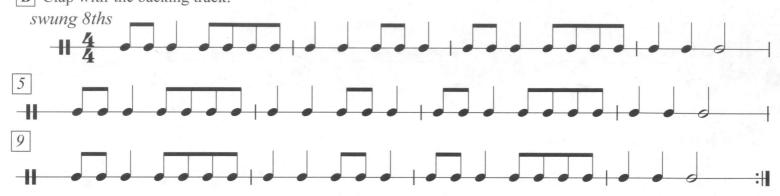

C 1. Play *without* the backing track.
   2. Play again *with* the backing track.

D 1. Play *without* the backing track.
   2. Play again *with* the backing track.

E 1. Play *without* the backing track.
2. Play again *with* the backing track.

* Improv notes:

* IMPROVISATION:
use this rhythm

* use the Improv notes in any order

Listen closely as you play your improvisation.
  - Does each note sound good with the backing track?
  - Are you keeping a steady beat and staying with the backing track?
Play several different improvisations and choose your favorite. Play it for your teacher.

✔ **Improv Tip:** *The "blues note" E♭ in your right hand should clash nicely with the E♮ in the chord*
in your left hand. Try it in several places in your improvisation.

Improv Etude - Trucking Along

MODULE 3

A Play the backing track of *Trucking Along*. The opening clicks represent ♩ (quarter notes).
After the clicks, clap ♩ with the track.

B Clap with the backing track:

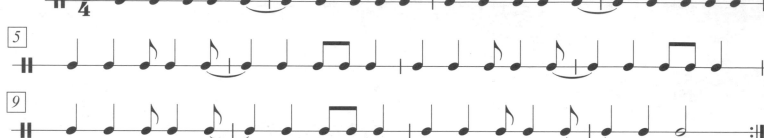

C 1. Play *without* the backing track.
2. Play again *with* the backing track.

D 1. Play *without* the backing track.
2. Play again *with* the backing track.

E 1. Play *without* the backing track.
2. Play again *with* the backing track.

* Improv notes:

swung 8ths

* IMPROVISATION:
use this rhythm

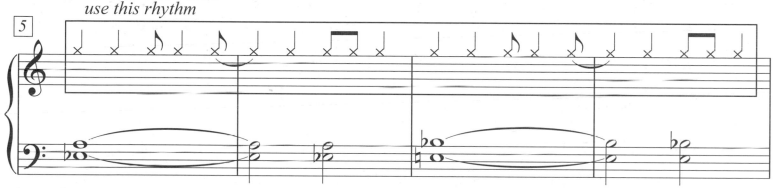

* use the Improv notes in any order

Listen closely as you play your improvisation.
  - Does each note sound good with the backing track?
  - Are you keeping a steady beat and staying with the backing track?
Play several different improvisations and choose your favorite. Play it for your teacher.

✔ **Improv Tip:** *The ties in the given rhythm add punch to your improvisation.*
           Experiment with accents and different articulation, too.

Improv Etude - Trucking Along

MODULE 4

A Play the backing track of *Trucking Along*. The opening clicks represent ♩ (quarter notes).

   After the clicks, clap ♩ with the track.

B Clap with the backing track:

C 1. Play *without* the backing track.
   2. Play again *with* the backing track.

D 1. Play *without* the backing track.
   2. Play again *with* the backing track.

E 1. Play *without* the backing track.
   2. Play again *with* the backing track.

* Improv notes:

* IMPROVISATION:
use this rhythm

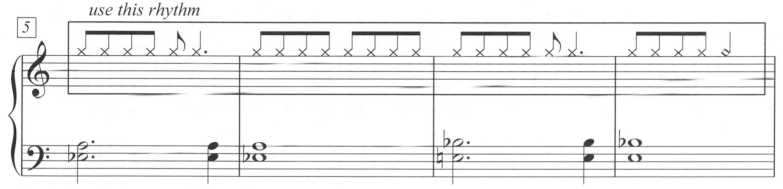

* use the Improv notes in any order

Listen closely as you play your improvisation.
   - Does each note sound good with the backing track?
   - Are you keeping a steady beat and staying with the backing track?
Play several different improvisations and choose your favorite. Play it for your teacher.

✔ **Improv Tip:** *A new note to consider using - E♮. It's not in the "Improv notes" but you*
                might find that it can work too! Experiment with where it sounds best.

Improv Etude - A Thing Of Beauty

MODULE 1

A Play the backing track of *A Thing Of Beauty*. The opening clicks represent ♩ (quarter notes). After the clicks, clap ♩ with the track.

B Clap with the backing track:

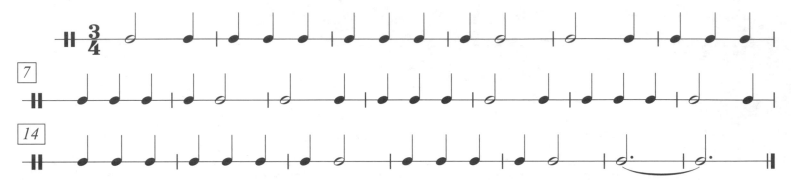

C 1. Play *without* the backing track.
    2. Play again *with* the backing track.

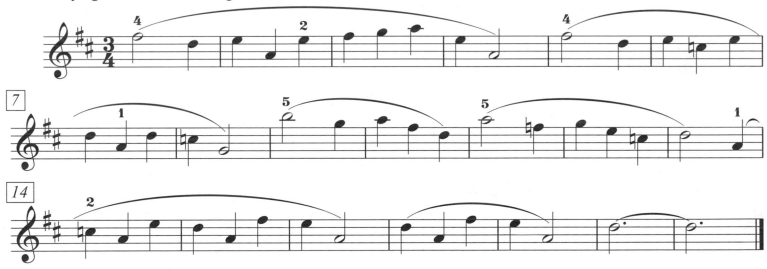

D 1. Play *without* the backing track.
    2. Play again *with* the backing track.

E 1. Play *without* the backing track.
2. Play again *with* the backing track.

* Improv notes:

* use the Improv notes in any order

IMPROVISATION: *use this rhythm*

IMPROVISATION:
use this rhythm

* use the Improv notes in any order

Listen closely as you play your improvisation.
- Does each note sound good with the backing track?
- Are you keeping a steady beat and staying with the backing track?
Play several different improvisations and choose your favorite. Play it for your teacher.

✔ **Improv Tip:** *A floating effect would be nice here. How might you achieve that in your improvisation? Consider articulation and accents as well as note choice.*

Improv Etude - A Thing Of Beauty

MODULE 2

A Play the backing track of *A Thing Of Beauty*. The opening clicks represent ♩ (quarter notes).

After the clicks, clap ♩ with the track.

B Clap with the backing track:

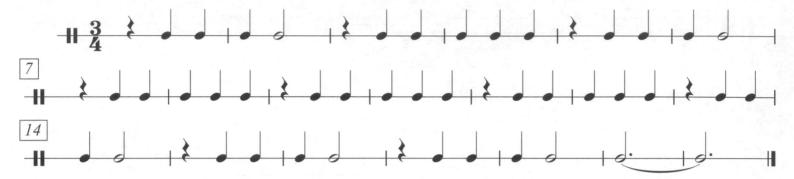

C 1. Play *without* the backing track.
2. Play again *with* the backing track.

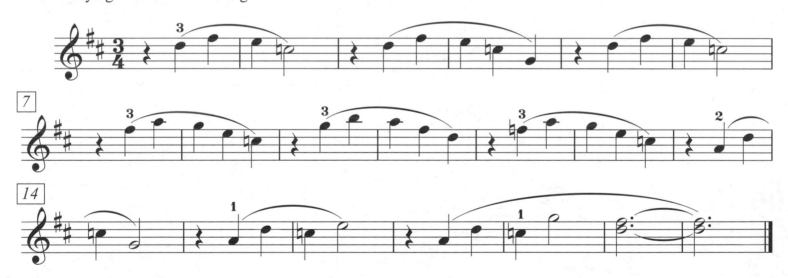

D 1. Play *without* the backing track.
2. Play again *with* the backing track.

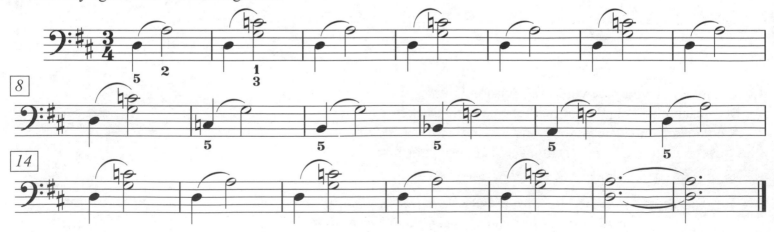

E 1. Play *without* the backing track.
2. Play again *with* the backing track.

* Improv notes:

* use the Improv notes in any order

* IMPROVISATION: *use this rhythm*

* IMPROVISATION:
use this rhythm

* use the Improv notes in any order

Listen closely as you play your improvisation.
- Does each note sound good with the backing track?
- Are you keeping a steady beat and staying with the backing track?
Play several different improvisations and choose your favorite. Play it for your teacher.

✔ **Improv Tip:** *Try creating a 'question and answer' like the one provided.*
How will you do that?

Improv Etude - A Thing Of Beauty

MODULE 3

A Play the backing track of *A Thing Of Beauty*. The opening clicks represent ♩ (quarter notes).
After the clicks, clap ♩ with the track.

B Clap with the backing track:
swung 8ths

C 1. Play *without* the backing track.
2. Play again *with* the backing track.

swung 8ths

D 1. Play *without* the backing track.
2. Play again *with* the backing track.

E 1. Play *without* the backing track.
   2. Play again *with* the backing track.

* Improv notes:

* use the Improv notes in any order

* IMPROVISATION: *use this rhythm*

* use the Improv notes in any order

Listen closely as you play your improvisation.
 - Does each note sound good with the backing track?
 - Are you keeping a steady beat and staying with the backing track?
Play several different improvisations and choose your favorite. Play it for your teacher.

✔ **Improv Tip:** *Should syncopated notes always have an accent? Try them accented and
then light and airy. See which suits the mood best.*

Improv Etude - A Thing Of Beauty

MODULE 4

A Play the backing track of *A Thing Of Beauty*. The opening clicks represent ♩ (quarter notes).
After the clicks, clap ♩ with the track.

B Clap with the backing track:
swung 8ths

C 1. Play *without* the backing track.
   2. Play again *with* the backing track.

swung 8ths

D 1. Play *without* the backing track.
   2. Play again *with* the backing track.

swung 8ths

E 1. Play *without* the backing track.
2. Play again *with* the backing track.

* Improv notes:

* use the Improv notes in any order

* IMPROVISATION: *use this rhythm*

* use the Improv notes in any order

Listen closely as you play your improvisation.
- Does each note sound good with the backing track?
- Are you keeping a steady beat and staying with the backing track?
Play several different improvisations and choose your favorite. Play it for your teacher.

✔ **Improv Tip:** *Adding passing tones between chord tones is a great improv technique.*

Improv Etude - A Matter Of Regret

MODULE 1

A Play the backing track of *A Matter Of Regret*. The opening clicks represent ♩ (quarter notes).

After the clicks, clap ♩ with the track.

B Clap with the backing track:

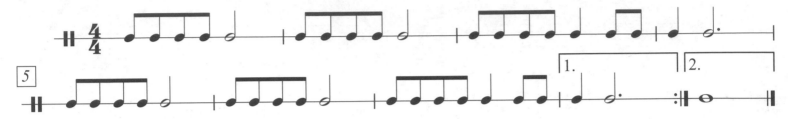

C 1. Play *without* the backing track.
2. Play again *with* the backing track.

D 1. Play *without* the backing track.
2. Play again *with* the backing track.

E 1. Play *without* the backing track.
  2. Play again *with* the backing track.

* Improv notes:

* IMPROVISATION:
  use this rhythm

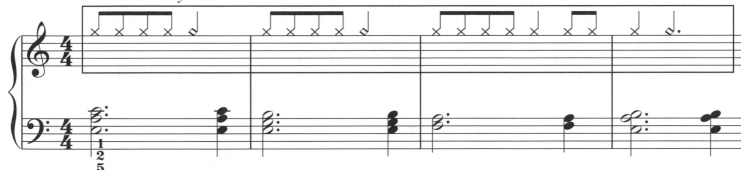

* use the Improv notes in any order

* IMPROVISATION: *use this rhythm*

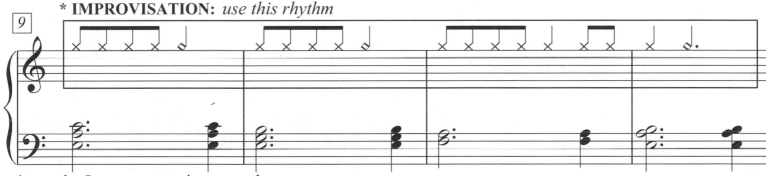

* use the Improv notes in any order

Listen closely as you play your improvisation.
  - Does each note sound good with the backing track?
  - Are you keeping a steady beat and staying with the backing track?
Play several different improvisations and choose your favorite. Play it for your teacher.

✔ **Improv Tip:** *Repetition and sequence are both great improvisation tools.*

Improv Etude - A Matter Of Regret

MODULE 2

A Play the backing track of *A Matter Of Regret*. The opening clicks represent ♩ (quarter notes).
After the clicks, clap ♩ with the track.

B Clap with the backing track:

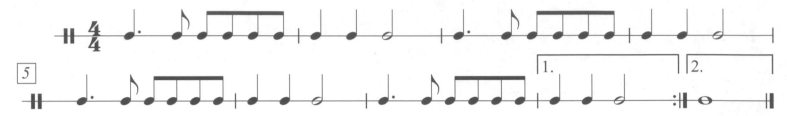

C 1. Play *without* the backing track.
2. Play again *with* the backing track.

D 1. Play *without* the backing track.
2. Play again *with* the backing track.

E 1. Play *without* the backing track.
2. Play again *with* the backing track.

* Improv notes:

* IMPROVISATION:
use this rhythm

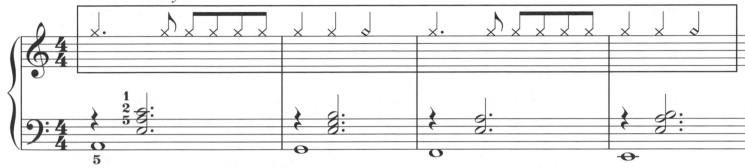

* use the Improv notes in any order

* IMPROVISATION:
use this rhythm

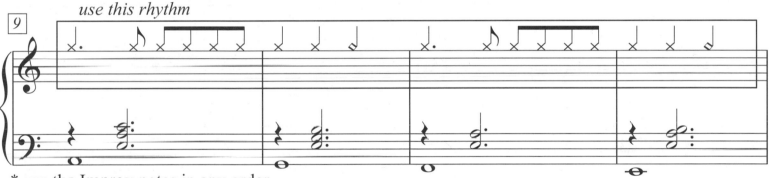

* use the Improv notes in any order

Listen closely as you play your improvisation.
- Does each note sound good with the backing track?
- Are you keeping a steady beat and staying with the backing track?
Play several different improvisations and choose your favorite. Play it for your teacher.

✔ Improv Tip: *Expressive melodies often have a vivid shape. Does yours?*

Improv Etude - A Matter Of Regret

MODULE 3

A Play the backing track of *A Matter Of Regret*. The opening clicks represent ♩ (quarter notes).
After the clicks, clap ♩ with the track.

B Clap with the backing track:

C 1. Play *without* the backing track.
2. Play again *with* the backing track.

D 1. Play *without* the backing track.
2. Play again *with* the backing track.

E 1. Play *without* the backing track.
2. Play again *with* the backing track.

* Improv notes:

* IMPROVISATION:
use this rhythm

* use the Improv notes in any order

* IMPROVISATION:
use this rhythm

* use the Improv notes in any order

Listen closely as you play your improvisation.
- Does each note sound good with the backing track?
- Are you keeping a steady beat and staying with the backing track?

Play several different improvisations and choose your favorite. Play it for your teacher.

✔ **Improv Tip:** *There are quite a few position changes in this module - make them smooth and expressive. It can be very effective to have melodies in contrasting registers.*

Improv Etude - A Matter Of Regret

MODULE 4

A Play the backing track of *A Matter Of Regret*. The opening clicks represent ♩ (quarter notes).
After the clicks, clap ♩ with the track.

B Clap with the backing track:

C 1. Play *without* the backing track.
2. Play again *with* the backing track.

D 1. Play *without* the backing track.
2. Play again *with* the backing track.

E 1. Play *without* the backing track.
2. Play again *with* the backing track.

* Improv notes:

* IMPROVISATION:
use this rhythm

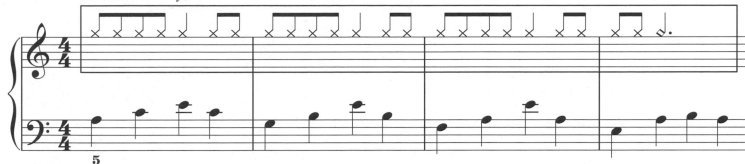

* use the Improv notes in any order

* IMPROVISATION:
use this rhythm

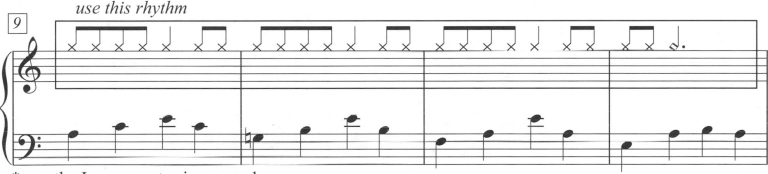

* use the Improv notes in any order

Listen closely as you play your improvisation.
- Does each note sound good with the backing track?
- Are you keeping a steady beat and staying with the backing track?
Play several different improvisations and choose your favorite. Play it for your teacher.

✔ **Improv Tip:** *Compare m. 15 to m. 7. How does the expansion of the intervals in the melody affect the sound?*

Improv Etude - Along The Coast

MODULE 1

A Play the backing track of *Along The Coast*. The opening clicks represent ♩ (quarter notes).
After the clicks, clap ♩ with the track.

B Clap with the backing track:

C 1. Play *without* the backing track.
2. Play again *with* the backing track.

D 1. Play *without* the backing track.
2. Play again *with* the backing track.

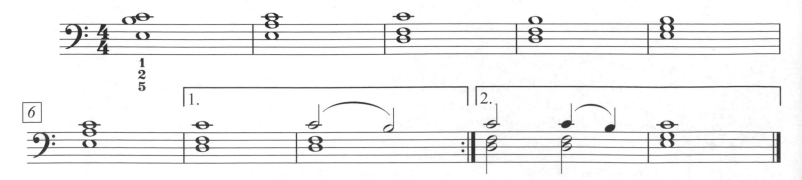

E 1. Play *without* the backing track.
2. Play again *with* the backing track.

* Improv notes:

* IMPROVISATION:
use this rhythm

* use the Improv notes in any order

Listen closely as you play your improvisation.
- Does each note sound good with the backing track?
- Are you keeping a steady beat and staying with the backing track?
Play several different improvisations and choose your favorite. Play it for your teacher.

✔ **Improv Tip:** *The notes to use for improvising cover quite a range.*
Play with both high and low melodies.

Improv Etude - Along The Coast

MODULE 2

A Play the backing track of *Along The Coast*. The opening clicks represent ♩ (quarter notes).
After the clicks, clap ♩ with the track.

B Clap with the backing track:

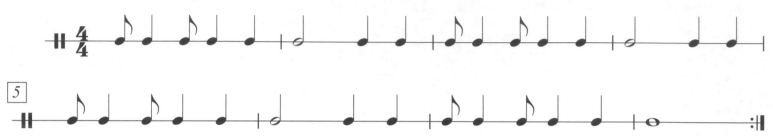

C 1. Play *without* the backing track.
2. Play again *with* the backing track.

D 1. Play *without* the backing track.
2. Play again *with* the backing track.

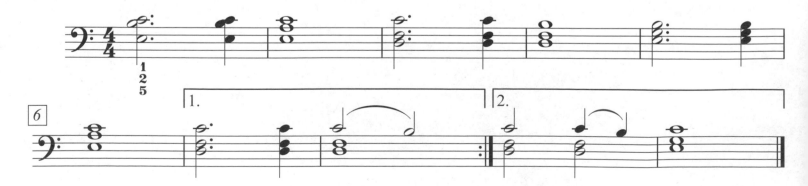

E 1. Play *without* the backing track.
2. Play again *with* the backing track.

* Improv notes:

* IMPROVISATION:
use this rhythm

* use the Improv notes in any order

Listen closely as you play your improvisation.
- Does each note sound good with the backing track?
- Are you keeping a steady beat and staying with the backing track?
Play several different improvisations and choose your favorite. Play it for your teacher.

✔ **Improv Tip:** *Notice how you can play the same melody starting a note higher.*
The same pattern on different notes is called a sequence.

Improv Etude - Along The Coast

MODULE 3

A Play the backing track of *Along The Coast*. The opening clicks represent ♩ (quarter notes).
After the clicks, clap ♩ with the track.

B Clap with the backing track:

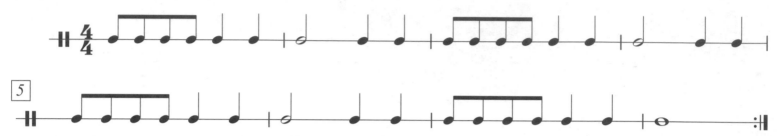

C 1. Play *without* the backing track.
2. Play again *with* the backing track.

D 1. Play *without* the backing track.
2. Play again *with* the backing track.

E 1. Play *without* the backing track.
2. Play again *with* the backing track.

* Improv notes:

* use the Improv notes in any order

Listen closely as you play your improvisation.
- Does each note sound good with the backing track?
- Are you keeping a steady beat and staying with the backing track?
Play several different improvisations and choose your favorite. Play it for your teacher.

✔ **Improv Tip:** *The classical sequence always has three statements of the musical idea, each starting on a different note. Does your improvised motif sound good played that way?*

Improv Etude - Along The Coast

MODULE 4

A Play the backing track of *Along The Coast*. The opening clicks represent ♩ (quarter notes).
After the clicks, clap ♩ with the track.

B Clap with the backing track:

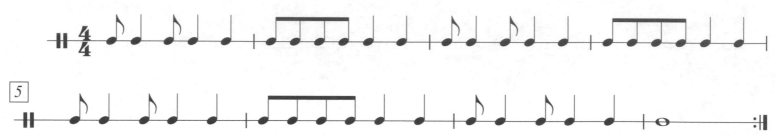

C 1. Play *without* the backing track.
2. Play again *with* the backing track.

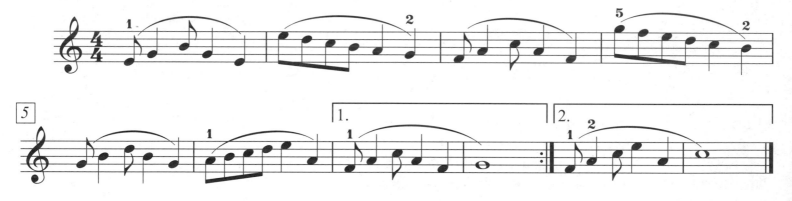

D 1. Play *without* the backing track.
2. Play again *with* the backing track.

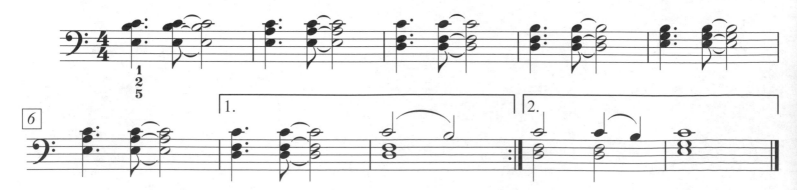

E 1. Play *without* the backing track.
2. Play again *with* the backing track.

* Improv notes:

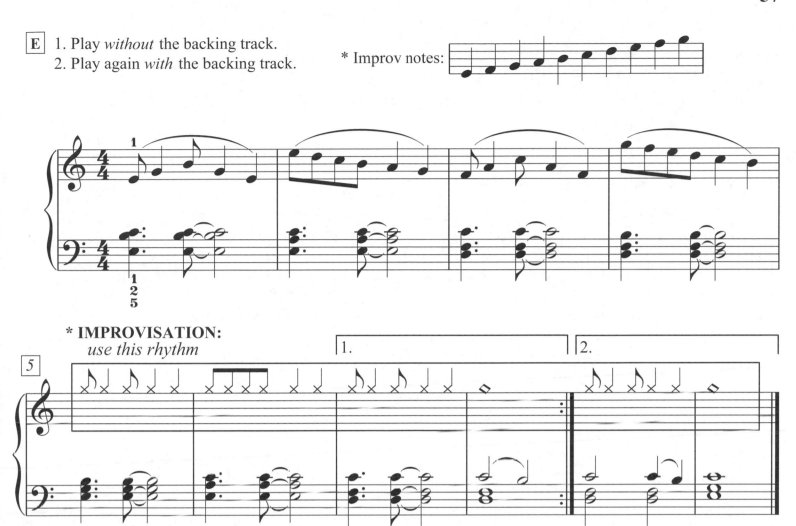

* **IMPROVISATION:**
use this rhythm

* use the Improv notes in any order

Listen closely as you play your improvisation.
- Does each note sound good with the backing track?
- Are you keeping a steady beat and staying with the backing track?
Play several different improvisations and choose your favorite. Play it for your teacher.

✔ **Improv Tip:** *You can create a "happier" effect by using jumps to the higher register.*

Improv Etude - Walking In The Sun

MODULE 1

A Play the backing track of *Walking In The Sun*. The opening clicks represent ♩ (quarter notes).

  After the clicks, clap ♩ with the track.

B Clap with the backing track:

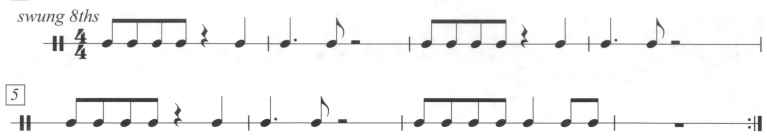

C 1. Play *without* the backing track.
   2. Play again *with* the backing track.

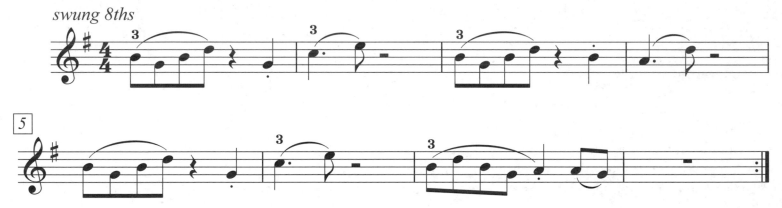

D 1. Play *without* the backing track.
   2. Play again *with* the backing track.

E 1. Play *without* the backing track.
2. Play again *with* the backing track.

* Improv notes:

swung 8ths

* IMPROVISATION:
  use this rhythm

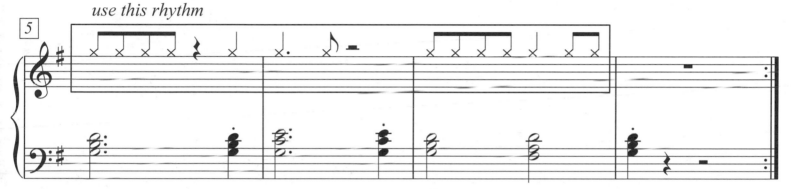

* use the Improv notes in any order

Listen closely as you play your improvisation.
  - Does each note sound good with the backing track?
  - Are you keeping a steady beat and staying with the backing track?
Play several different improvisations and choose your favorite. Play it for your teacher.

✔ **Improv Tip:** *Repetition works well when the rhythm is tricky.*

Improv Etude - Walking In The Sun

MODULE 2

A Play the backing track of *Walking In The Sun*. The opening clicks represent ♩ (quarter notes).
After the clicks, clap ♩ with the track.

B Clap with the backing track:

swung 8ths

C 1. Play *without* the backing track.
2. Play again *with* the backing track.

swung 8ths

D 1. Play *without* the backing track.
2. Play again *with* the backing track.

swung 8ths

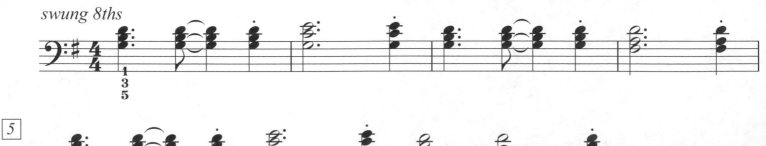

E 1. Play *without* the backing track.
2. Play again *with* the backing track.

* Improv notes:

swung 8ths

* IMPROVISATION:
use this rhythm

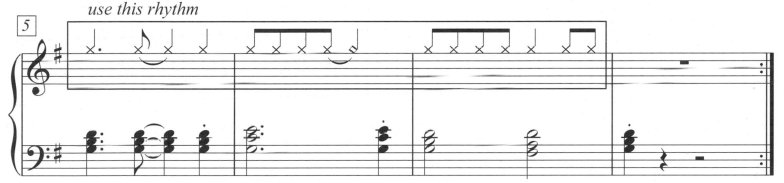

* use the Improv notes in any order

Listen closely as you play your improvisation.
- Does each note sound good with the backing track?
- Are you keeping a steady beat and staying with the backing track?
Play several different improvisations and choose your favorite. Play it for your teacher.

✔ **Improv Tip:** *A steady beat is critical to this piece. Rhythm first!*

Improv Etude - Walking In The Sun

MODULE 3

A Play the backing track of *Walking In The Sun.* The opening clicks represent ♩ (quarter notes).

After the clicks, clap ♩ with the track.

B Clap with the backing track:

C 1. Play *without* the backing track.
2. Play again *with* the backing track.

D 1. Play *without* the backing track.
2. Play again *with* the backing track.

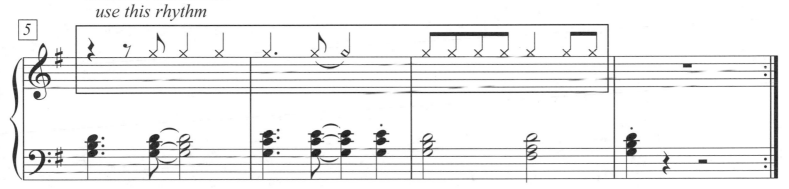

E 1. Play *without* the backing track.
2. Play again *with* the backing track.

* Improv notes:

swung 8ths

* IMPROVISATION:
use this rhythm

* use the Improv notes in any order

Listen closely as you play your improvisation.
- Does each note sound good with the backing track?
- Are you keeping a steady beat and staying with the backing track?

Play several different improvisations and choose your favorite. Play it for your teacher.

✔ **Improv Tip:** *When you play the improvisation section without the backing it should still sound very satisfying. Try inverting (turning upside down) some of the melodic ideas.*

Improv Etude - Walking In The Sun

MODULE 4

A Play the backing track of *Walking In The Sun*. The opening clicks represent ♩ (quarter notes).
After the clicks, clap ♩ with the track.

B Clap with the backing track:
swung 8ths

C 1. Play *without* the backing track.
2. Play again *with* the backing track.

swung 8ths

D 1. Play *without* the backing track.
2. Play again *with* the backing track.

swung 8ths

E 1. Play *without* the backing track.
    2. Play again *with* the backing track.

* Improv notes:

* IMPROVISATION:
use this rhythm

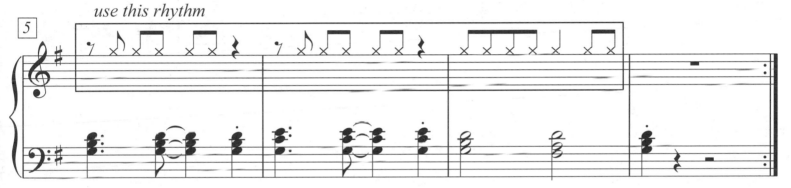

* use the Improv notes in any order

Listen closely as you play your improvisation.
  - Does each note sound good with the backing track?
  - Are you keeping a steady beat and staying with the backing track?
Play several different improvisations and choose your favorite. Play it for your teacher.

✔ **Improv Tip:** *In certain types of jazz and pop, a melodic idea is called a "lick".*
  How many licks do you see in mm. 1-4? Use the same number in your improvisation.

Performance Etude - Rockin' In The Aisles

A Practice the *Rockin' In The Aisles* Performance Etude based on the notes and rhythms you have already used in the modules. Once this feels comfortable, experiment with your own rhythms. Do this several times.

Improv notes:

B Work on your improvisation without the backing track until you can play with a steady tempo. Then practice with the backing track. Choose your favorite version and play it for your teacher.

Listen closely as you play your improvisation.
- Does each note sound good with the backing track?
- Are you keeping a steady beat and staying with the backing track?

✔ **Improv Tip:** *Remember - when the lh pattern gets complicated, the rh will usually sound better if it's simple.*

Performance Etude - Going For It

A Practice the *Going For It* Performance Etude based on
the notes and rhythms you have already used in the modules.
Once this feels comfortable, experiment with your own rhythms.
Do this several times.

Improv notes:

B Work on your improvisation without the backing track until you can play with a steady tempo.
Then practice with the backing track. Choose your favorite version and play it for your teacher.

Listen closely as you play your improvisation.
- Does each note sound good with the backing track?
- Are you keeping a steady beat and staying with the backing track?

✔ **Improv Tip:** *Basing your improvisation on chord tones is a good way to start.*
But add some non-harmonic tones, too!

Performance Etude - A Knight's Tale

68

A Practice the *A Knight's Tale* Performance Etude based on
the notes and rhythms you have already used in the modules.
Once this feels comfortable, experiment with your own rhythms.
Do this several times.

Improv notes:

B Work on your improvisation without the backing track until you can play with a steady tempo.
Then practice with the backing track. Choose your favorite version and play it for your teacher.

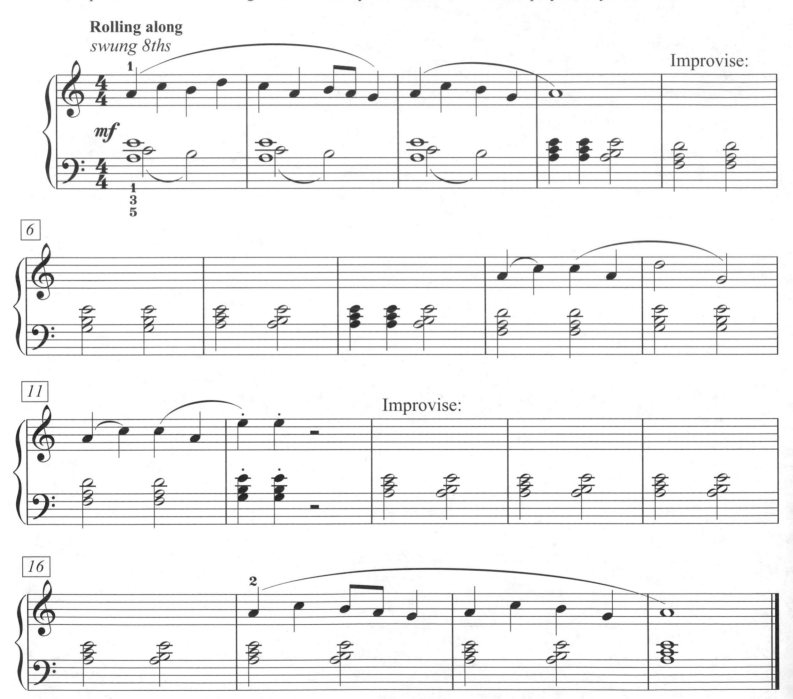

Listen closely as you play your improvisation.
- Does each note sound good with the backing track?
- Are you keeping a steady beat and staying with the backing track?

✔ **Improv Tip:** *This piece has a graceful character, so keep the right hand melodies smooth and flowing.*

Performance Etude - Trucking Along

A Practice the *Trucking Along* Performance Etude based on
the notes and rhythms you have already used in the modules.
Once this feels comfortable, experiment with your own rhythms.
Do this several times.

Improv notes:

B Work on your improvisation without the backing track until you can play with a steady tempo.
Then practice with the backing track. Choose your favorite version and play it for your teacher.

Listen closely as you play your improvisation.
- Does each note sound good with the backing track?
- Are you keeping a steady beat and staying with the backing track?

☑ **Improv Tip:** *See where you can slip in the occasional right hand E♮.*
This will create more contrast in your performance.

Performance Etude - A Thing Of Beauty

Improv notes:

A Practice the *A Thing Of Beauty* Performance Etude based on
the notes and rhythms you have already used in the modules.
Once this feels comfortable, experiment with your own rhythms.
Do this several times.

B Work on your improvisation without the backing track until you can play with a steady tempo.
Then practice with the backing track. Choose your favorite version and play it for your teacher.

Listen closely as you play your improvisation.
- Does each note sound good with the backing track?
- Are you keeping a steady beat and staying with the backing track?

✔ **Improv Tip:** *Aim for simplicity and beauty of sound when you improvise.*

Performance Etude - A Matter Of Regret

A Practice the *A Matter Of Regret* Performance Etude based on the notes and rhythms you have already used in the modules. Once this feels comfortable, experiment with your own rhythms. Do this several times.

Improv notes:

B Work on your improvisation without the backing track until you can play with a steady tempo. Then practice with the backing track. Choose your favorite version and play it for your teacher.

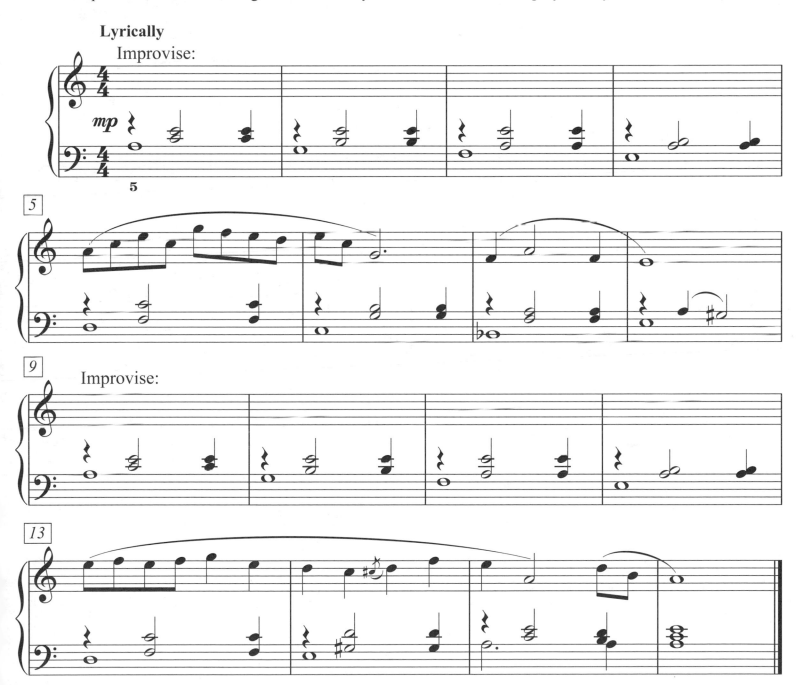

Listen closely as you play your improvisation.
- Does each note sound good with the backing track?
- Are you keeping a steady beat and staying with the backing track?

☑ **Improv Tip:** *Create an expressive two-measure melody and answer it with a contrasting two-measure melody.*

Performance Etude - Along The Coast

Improv notes:

A Practice the *Along The Coast* Performance Etude based on
the notes and rhythms you have already used in the modules.
Once this feels comfortable, experiment with your own rhythms.
Do this several times.

B Work on your improvisation without the backing track until you can play with a steady tempo.
Then practice with the backing track. Choose your favorite version and play it for your teacher.

Listen closely as you play your improvisation.
- Does each note sound good with the backing track?
- Are you keeping a steady beat and staying with the backing track?

✔ **Improv Tip:** *You can add passing tones or neighboring tones to your improvisation.*
They'll all sound good over the rich harmonies in the left-hand chords.

Performance Etude - Walking In The Sun

A Practice the *Walking In The Sun* Performance Etude based on the notes and rhythms you have already used in the modules. Once this feels comfortable, experiment with your own rhythms. Do this several times.

Improv notes:

B Work on your improvisation without the backing track until you can play with a steady tempo. Then practice with the backing track. Choose your favorite version and play it for your teacher.

Listen closely as you play your improvisation.
- Does each note sound good with the backing track?
- Are you keeping a steady beat and staying with the backing track?

☑ **Improv Tip:** *Pay attention to details and make it fun!*

Allegro

C. Czerny

Moderato

C. Gurlitt

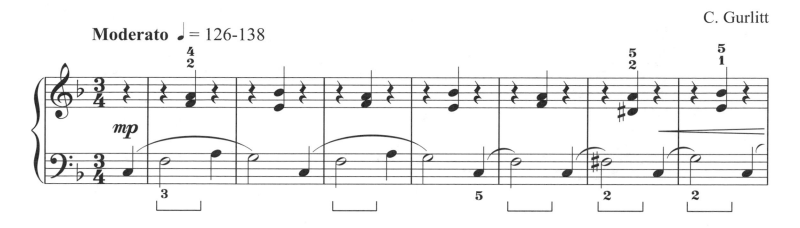

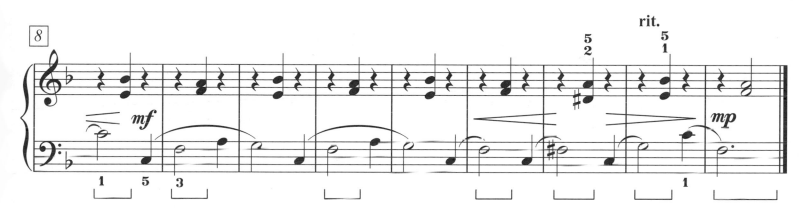

Moderato - no. 1

C. Stamaty

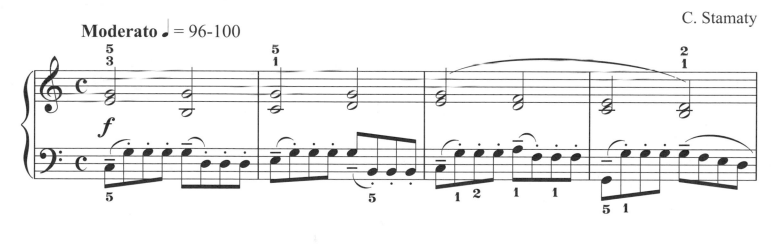

Moderato

F. Beyer

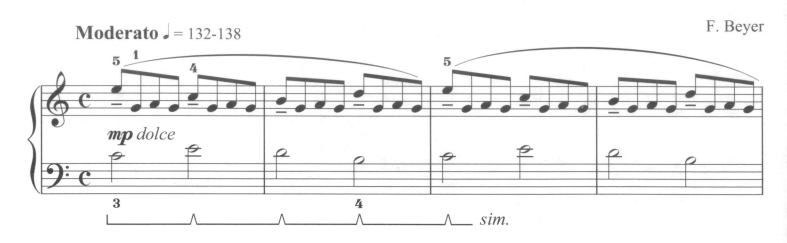

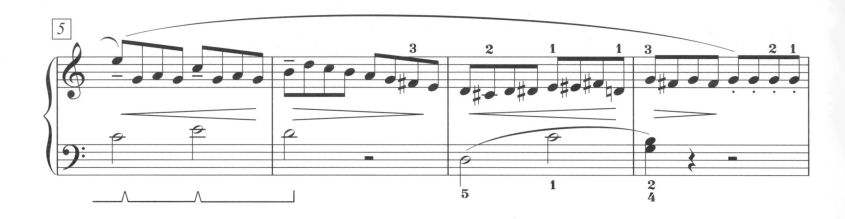

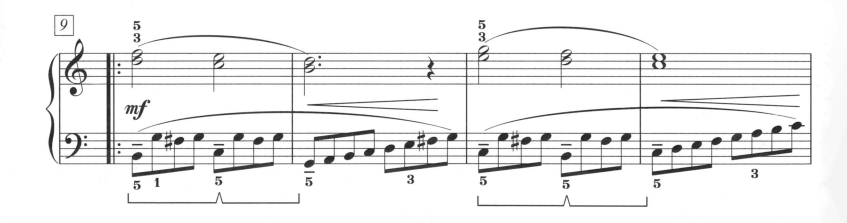

Allegretto

H. Lemoine

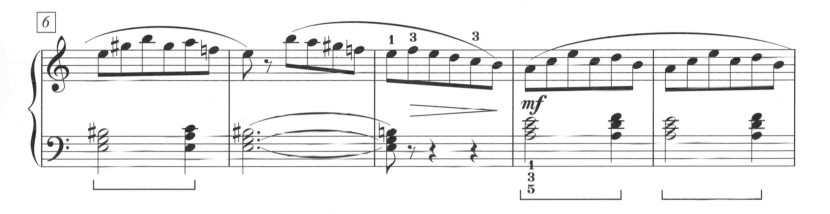

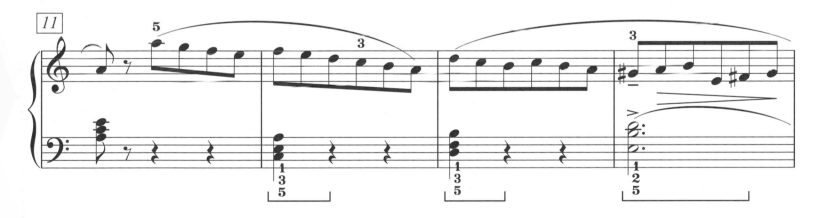

Moderato - no. 2

Stamaty

Tempo di Valse

C.A. Loeschhorn

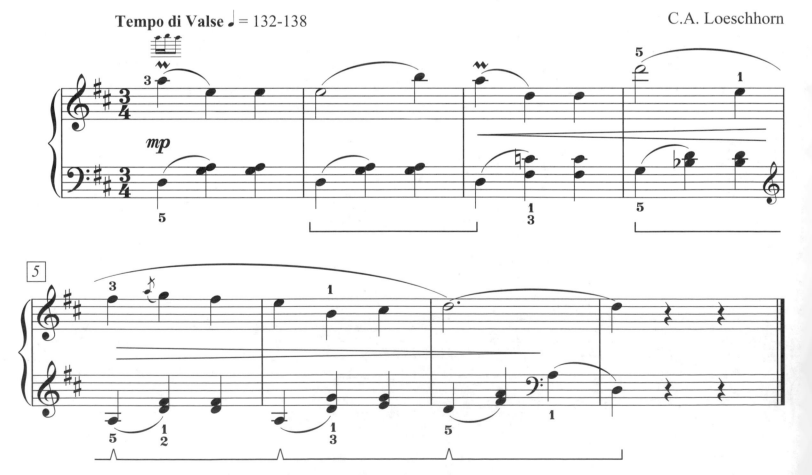

Andante

C. Gurlitt

Drifting

Christopher Norton

Taking Turns

Christopher Norton

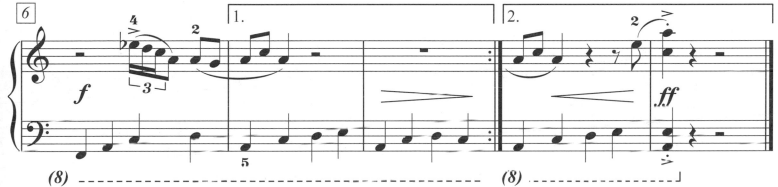

Stick Dance

Christopher Norton

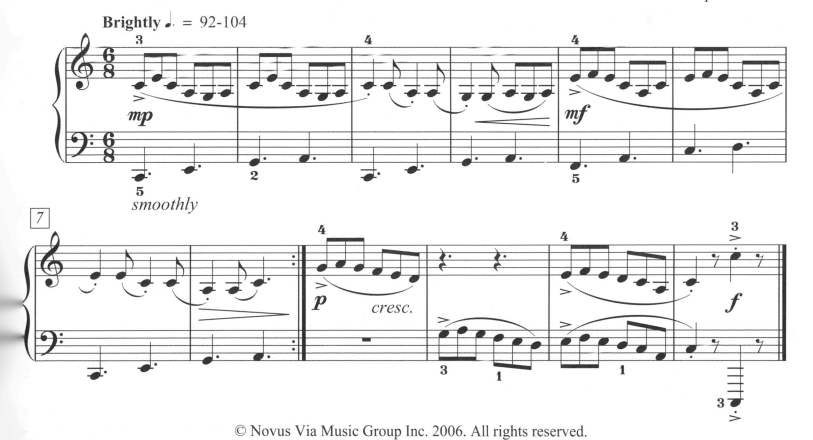

Brooding

Christopher Norton

Feather Duster

Christopher Norton

Snakes On A Train

Christopher Norton

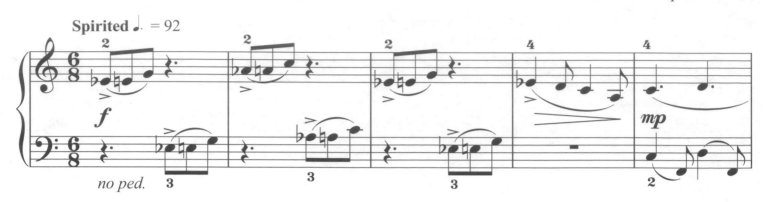

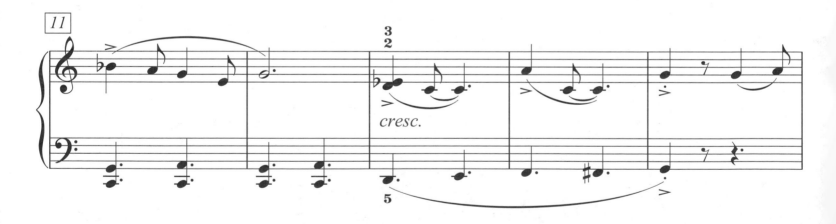

Gathering Pace

Christopher Norton

LEVEL 4 ETUDES
Glossary

Backbeat . . . . Emphasis on beats 2 and 4, in a 4-beat bar. Usually accented by the drums, the backbeat is the most common rhythm in rock music.

Blues . . . . Musical genre created by African-American musicians, with "blues" notes played against a major-key chord progression often using chords I, IV and V. Examples include: *Heartbreak Hotel*

Blues notes . . . . A pattern based on a major scale with flat 3rd, 5th, and 7th notes.

Bossa nova . . . . A Brazilian dance style, with a 2+3+3 eighth note pattern in the right hand over a dotted quarter note, eighth note pattern in the left hand, often with rich, sensuous chords. Examples include: *The Girl from Ipanema*

Call and . . . . A style of singing in which the
response melody sung by one singer is echoed or "answered" by another. Examples include: *My Generation*

Calypso . . . . A popular song form from the Caribbean island of Trinidad, generally upbeat. Popularized by Harry Belafonte, calypso has an emphasis on acoustic guitars and a variety of percussion instruments, particularly claves, shaker, and bongos. Examples include: *Walking in the Sun, Banana Boat Song*

Cha cha . . . . An exciting syncopated Latin dance, with a characteristic "cha cha cha" rhythm at the end. Examples include: *Never on a Sunday*

Country Swing . A combination of country, cowboy, polka, and folk music, blended with a jazzy "swing", featuring pedal steel guitar. Examples include: *Lovesick Blues* (Hank Williams)

8-beat rock . . . . A staple rock 'n' roll rhythmic pattern with 8 eighth notes in every bar featuring strong accents on beats 2 and 4. The accents are usually emphasized by the drums.

Funk (funky) . . . A musical style associated with James Brown. The bass features 16th note pickups to the beat, with flourishes of 16th note syncopations in the bass and horns against a rock backbeat. Examples include: *Get on Up*

Gospel . . . . An African-American religious style featuring a solo singer with heavily ornamented, simple melodies and a dramatic, wide vocal range. The soloist is often accompanied by a choir providing a rich harmonic backdrop. Examples include: *Nobody Knows the Trouble I've Seen*

Hoedown . . . . . . The music for a square dance. Hoedowns often feature fiddle as a lead instrument, having roots in Scottish and Irish folk music (see Irish Jig), but you would also expect to find banjo, accordion, and perhaps an upright bass. Many hoedowns get faster and faster in order to whip up excitement for the dancers. Examples include: *Take Your Partners, Hoedown from Rodeo* (Copland)

Impressionist . . A style of the late 19th and early 20th centuries, using untraditional harmonies and rhythms to evoke a mood or place. Famous composers include Debussy, Ravel, Duke Ellington, and Bill Evans. Examples include: *Ripples on the Water, Claire de Lune, Waltz for Debby* (Bill Evans)

Irish Jig . . . . A lively dance in triple time, generally led by tin whistle and fiddle. Examples include: *The Rambler*

Jazz . . . . Jazz encompasses New Orleans Dixieland from the early 1900's, New York stride piano of the 1930's, big-band music from the 1940's, Chicago blues of the 1950's, and atonal free-form music of the 1960's. Jazz has its origins in uniquely American musical traditions, is generally based on chord structures of popular songs from the 1920's to the present, and always features some improvisation.

Jazz waltz . . . . . . A generally relaxed swing style in 3/4 time. Examples include: *Tenderly, My Favorite Things*

Leroy Brown . . An easy-going shuffle style
feel popularized by a Jim Croce song of the same name. Examples include: *Trucking Along, Leroy Brown*

Motown . . . . A style of soul music which originated in Detroit, whose features include the use of tambourine along with drums and a "call and response" singing style derived from gospel music. Examples include: *Motor City, ABC*

Off-beat . . . . An accented note, motif, or phrase played on a normally unaccented beat.

Pop ballad . . . . . A form of slow love song prevalent in nearly all genres of popular music. There are various types of pop ballad, from sixteenth-note ballads, to eight-beat ballads, to swing ballads. There is generally an emphasis on romance in the lyrics. Examples include: *A Matter of Regret, Kiss from a Rose*

Reggae . . . . A music style from Jamaica, with elements of calypso, rhythm and blues, and characterized by a strong offbeat. Examples include: *Jamaican Market, No Woman No Cry*

Rhythm . . . . A style of music that combines blues and jazz, characterized by a strong off-beat and variations on syncopated instrumental phrases.

Shuffle . . . . Based on the tap dancing style where the dancer, wearing soft-soled shoes, "shuffles" their feet in a swung 8ths rhythm. Examples include: *Train Stop, Lido Shuffle*

16-beat ballad . A song-based style with gentle momentum created by continuous 16th notes in the rhythm, usually provided by the hi-hat cymbal. Examples include: *Killing Me Softly*

Soul . . . . An African-American style combining elements of gospel music and rhythm and blues.

Swing . . . . A fun, dance-like style, usually using swung 8ths.

Swung 8ths . . . . 8th notes that are written normally, but played in this gentle dotted rhythm:

Syncopation . . . An emphasis on weak beats and/or rests on strong beats to briefly change the pattern of metrical accents normally found in a time signature.

Tango . . . . A rhythmically strict style, with no off-beat and a snare roll on beat 4. Examples include: *Conquistador, Phantom of the Opera Tango*

Thriller feel . . . . Named after the title song on Michael Jackson's Thriller album, this style has a distinctive bass line and rhythmic feel. The funky bass plays against an 8-beat rock rhythm in a minor key. Examples include: *Ready for Action, Thriller*

Waltz . . . . A dance in 3/4 time, usually played with a strong accent on the first beat, with weaker beats on beats 2 and 3 in the accompaniment. Examples include: *Edelweiss*